AS A MAN THINKETH

Complete and Annotated

Includes
Commentary, Historical Context and
the Life of James Allen

James Allen

Ollie D. Orwell

AS A MAN THINKETH

Complete and Annotated

Includes
Commentary, Historical Context
and the Life of James Allen

James Allen

Ollie D. Orwell

As a Man Thinketh

James Allen

Commentary, annotations
and appendices by
Ollie D. Orwell

KING SOLOMON

ENTREACACIAS, SL
[Publishing House] Covadonga 8
33002 Oviedo - Asturias (Spain)
First edition: June 2025
ISBN: 978-84-18938-26-9

CONTENTS

The Quiet Magic of *As a Man Thinketh* 13
Foreword 19
Thought and Character 23
Effect of Thought on Circumstances 29
Effect of Thought on Health and the Body 45
Thought and Purpose 51
The Thought-Factor in Achievement 57
Visions and Ideals 65
Serenity 73
James Allen's *As a Man Thinketh* (1903):
Historical Context and Long-Term Relevance 79

Setting the Stage: Britain in 1903 and
the New Thought Movement 79
From Obscurity to Inspiration:
The Book's Reception and Legacy 87

James Allen: A Life Shaped by Thought 92

Early Years: Roots in Hardship and Hope 92
Self-Education and Spiritual Searching 93
Marriage and Literary Beginnings 94
As a Man Thinketh: The Breakthrough 94
The Philosopher of Ilfracombe 95
Legacy and Enduring Influence 96

Mind is the Master power that moulds and makes,
And Man is Mind, and evermore he takes
The tool of Thought, and, shaping what he wills,
Brings forth a thousand joys, a thousand ills:—
He thinks in secret, and it comes to pass:
Environment is but his looking-glass.

The Quiet Magic of *As a Man Thinketh*

Why a 1903 Pamphlet Still Works

"Men do not attract that which they want,
but that which they are."
— James Allen, 1903

More than a century after it first slipped quietly into print, *As a Man Thinketh* continues to circulate like a well-kept secret—passed from entrepreneur to athlete, from monk to manager, from parent to teenager discovering self-help for the first time. What accounts for its staying power? The pages that follow trace the unlikely journey of this pocket-sized essay, exploring how a single idea—*thought shapes destiny*—has threaded its way from Edwardian England through New Thought salons, mid-century success manuals, and today's neuroscience labs. In doing so, we will see why James Allen's humble booklet refuses to grow old, why it slips so easily into new vocabularies, and why its gentle imperative still sounds like a personal whisper amidst the 24-hour noise of modern life.

Here are some of the reasons why its quiet magic continues to work.

1 A SEED IDEA THAT NEVER WILTS

As a Man Thinketh is only a few thousand words long, yet its central premise—that thought is causal—has proved inexhaustible. Every generation rediscovers the essay because it answers a primal question: *How much of my life can I truly shape?* When Allen published the booklet for one shilling, he offered no seven-step program, no secret ritual—just a single, crystalline thesis. The idea is lean enough to slip into any era's vocabulary without losing its bite: swap "thought" for "coding," "mindset," or "mental model," and the sentence still hums.

2 FROM PROVERBS TO NEUROPLASTICITY

Allen quoted Proverbs 23:7; today neuroscientists speak of neuroplasticity—the brain's ability to re-wire itself along the grooves of repeated thought. Modern writers routinely note how Allen's maxim foreshadows lab findings on attention, cortical remapping, and mindset interventions. One recent commentary argues that the book "aligns with modern neuroplasticity" by showing how serenity and self-control reshape behavior patterns.

That continuity—Bible verse → Victorian pamphlet → fMRI scan—makes the work feel prophetic rather than dated.

3 A CROSS-CULTURAL CHORUS

Allen distilled a theme sung by multiple traditions:

Stoicism	*"The soul becomes dyed with the colour of its thoughts."* — Marcus Aurelius
Buddhism	*"All that we are is the result of what we have thought."* — *Dhammapada*
Cognitive-Behavioral Therapy	Change feelings by disputing and reframing thoughts.

By refusing sectarian labels, Allen lets each reader supply their own lineage. A practicing Buddhist, a Christian preacher, and a CBT therapist can all quote the pamphlet and feel perfectly orthodox.

4 NEW THOUGHT → POSITIVE PSYCHOLOGY → EVERYDAY LIFE

Victorian New Thought circles took Allen literally: right thinking cures disease. Mid-century success literature—Napoleon Hill, Norman Vincent Peale—softened the metaphysics but kept the optimism. Today's positive-psychology research asks what habits cultivate flourishing; bloggers still cite Allen as "an unmoving beacon" amid passing fads. The language evolves; the root metaphor—*garden the mind, harvest the life*—remains.

5 FORM FOLLOWS FUNCTION

Because the original booklet was pocket-sized, readers used it like a rosary: open anywhere, read a line, return to work. Its portability anticipated the way we now consume wisdom in phone-sized chunks. The prose, meanwhile, is lapidary: short sentences, concrete images (soil, seed, fruit). Strip away Edwardian phrasing and you have Twitter-ready aphorisms that travel well in a meme economy.

6 ELASTIC ENOUGH TO SURVIVE CULTURAL SHIFTS

- Industrial Age: a manual for self-made clerks.
- Depression Era: a tonic for scarcity thinking.
- Digital Era: a focus aid in the age of distraction.
- AI Era: a reminder that the *human* OS is still governed by attention loops.

Because Allen focuses on *process* (how thought shapes experience) rather than *content* (what to think about politics, diet, investments), the essay never locks itself to a single zeitgeist.

7 THREE REASONS THE SPELL ENDURES

1. Radical Responsibility
   Allen tells readers they are not passengers but

pilots—a flattering, bracing claim that survives every cultural turn toward fatalism.

2. Moral Minimalism
   No jargon, no doctrine, only cause-and-effect. The simplicity invites ownership rather than dependence on a guru.

3. Literary Stickiness
   Metaphors of gardening and harvest lodge in memory; they don't need footnotes or updates.

8 A LIVING CLASSIC

A century on, *As a Man Thinketh* continues to outsell trendier hardbacks. Business coaches assign it; meditation apps quote it; TikTok creators recite it over lo-fi beats. Critics may call it naïve, yet readers still test the experiment: clean up the inner dialogue for thirty days and watch outer circumstances shift. Enough find the promise confirmed to keep the little book in print, shared from mentor to mentee like a well-worn key.

In the end, the "magic" is not supernatural. It is the quiet alchemy that occurs whenever a concise truth meets a willing mind. Allen's pamphlet has simply proven to be an unusually fine conductor of that current—small, bright, and endlessly rechargeable.

FOREWORD

THIS little volume (the result of meditation and experience) is not intended as an exhaustive treatise on the much-written-upon subject of the power of thought. It is suggestive rather than explanatory, its object being to stimulate men and women to the discovery and perception of the truth that—

"They themselves are makers of themselves."

by virtue of the thoughts, which they choose and encourage; that mind is the master-weaver, both of the inner garment of character and the outer garment of circumstance, and that, as they may have hitherto woven in ignorance and pain they may now weave in enlightenment and happiness.

James Allen.
Broad Park Avenue,
Ilfracombe,
England

As a man thinketh in his heart so is he.

—JAMES ALLEN.

THOUGHT
AND
CHARACTER

THE aphorism, "As a man thinketh in his heart so is he,"[1] not only embraces the whole of a man's being, but is so comprehensive as to reach out to every condition and circumstance of his life. A man is literally *what he thinks,* his character being the complete sum of all his thoughts.

As the plant springs from, and could not be without, the seed, so every act of a man springs from the hidden seeds of thought, and could not have appeared without them. This applies equally to those acts called "spontaneous" and "unpremeditated" as to those, which are deliberately executed.

Act is the blossom of thought, and joy and suffering are its fruits; thus does a man garner in the sweet and bitter fruitage of his own husbandry.

"Thought in the mind hath made us, What we are
By thought was wrought and built. If a man's mind

[1] This aphorism is derived from *Proverbs 23:7* in the King James Bible. While modern translations often rephrase or contextualize the passage differently, the KJV version was widely known and frequently quoted in Allen's time. It serves as the title and thematic anchor of the book.

Hath evil thoughts, pain comes on him as comes
The wheel the ox behind....
..If one endure
In purity of thought, joy follows him
As his own shadow—sure."[2]

Man is a growth by law, and not a creation by artifice, and cause and effect is as absolute and undeviating in the hidden realm of thought as in the world of visible and material things. A noble and Godlike character is not a thing of favour or chance, but is the natural result of continued effort in right thinking, the effect of long-cherished association with Godlike thoughts. An ignoble and bestial character, by the same process, is the result of the continued harbouring of grovelling thoughts.

Man is made or unmade by himself; in the armoury of thought he forges the weapons by which he destroys himself; he also fashions the tools with which he builds for himself heavenly mansions of joy[3] and strength and peace. By the right choice and true application of

[2] This poetic excerpt paraphrases the *Dhammapada*, a foundational Buddhist scripture. The original verse (Dhp 1–2) states: *"All that we are is the result of what we have thought. If a man speaks or acts with an evil thought, pain follows him... If a man speaks or acts with a pure thought, happiness follows him like a shadow that never leaves him."*

[3] Likely a reference to *John 14:2*: *"In my Father's house are many mansions."* Allen reinterprets this Christian promise in psychological and metaphorical terms, suggesting that spiritual "mansions" are inner states constructed by thought.

thought, man ascends to the Divine Perfection; by the abuse and wrong application of thought, he descends below the level of the beast. Between these two extremes are all the grades of character, and man is their maker and master.

Of all the beautiful truths pertaining to the soul which have been restored and brought to light in this age, none is more gladdening or fruitful of divine promise and confidence than this—that man is the master of thought, the moulder of character, and the maker and shaper of condition, environment, and destiny.

As a being of Power, Intelligence, and Love, and the lord of his own thoughts, man holds the key to every situation, and contains within himself that transforming and regenerative agency by which he may make himself what he wills.

Man is always the master, even in his weaker and most abandoned state; but in his weakness and degradation he is the foolish master who misgoverns his "household." When he begins to reflect upon his condition, and to search diligently for the Law upon which his being is established, he then becomes the wise master, directing his energies with intelligence, and fashioning his thoughts to fruitful issues. Such is the *conscious* master, and man can only thus become by discovering *within himself* the laws of thought; which discovery is totally a matter of application, self analysis, and experience.

Only by much searching and mining, are gold and diamonds obtained, and man can find every truth connected with his being, if he will dig deep into the mine of his soul; and that he is the maker of his character, the moulder of his life, and the builder of his destiny, he may unerringly prove, if he will watch, control, and alter his thoughts, tracing their effects upon himself, upon others, and upon his life and circumstances, linking cause and effect by patient practice and investigation, and utilizing his every experience, even to the most trivial, everyday occurrence, as a means of obtaining that knowledge of himself which is Understanding, Wisdom, Power. In this direction, as in no other, is the law absolute that "He that seeketh findeth; and to him that knocketh it shall be opened;" for only by patience, practice, and ceaseless importunity can a man enter the Door of the Temple of Knowledge.

EFFECT OF THOUGHT
ON
CIRCUMSTANCES

MAN'S mind may be likened to a garden, which may be intelligently cultivated or allowed to run wild; but whether cultivated or neglected, it must, and will, *bring forth.* If no useful seeds are *put* into it, then an abundance of useless weed-seeds will *fall* therein, and will continue to produce their kind.

Just as a gardener cultivates his plot, keeping it free from weeds, and growing the flowers and fruits which he requires, so may a man tend the garden of his mind, weeding out all the wrong, useless, and impure thoughts, and cultivating toward perfection the flowers and fruits of right, useful, and pure thoughts. By pursuing this process, a man sooner or later discovers that he is the master-gardener of his soul[4], the director of his life. He also

[4] Possibly an allusion to the Christian notion of the *soul as vineyard* (cf. *Isaiah 5*) and the New Testament's repeated exhortations to *"keep watch over your heart."* The expression also reflects 19th-century Romantic notions of individual self-cultivation.

reveals, within himself, the laws of thought, and understands, with ever-increasing accuracy, how the thought-forces and mind elements operate in the shaping of his character, circumstances, and destiny.

Thought and character are one, and as character can only manifest and discover itself through environment and circumstance, the outer conditions of a person's life will always be found to be harmoniously related to his inner state. This does not mean that a man's circumstances at any given time are an indication of his *entire* character, but that those circumstances are so intimately connected with some vital thought-element within himself that, for the time being, they are indispensable to his development.

Every man is where he is by the law of his being; the thoughts which he has built into his character have brought him there, and in the arrangement of his life there is no element of chance, but all is the result of a law which cannot err. This is just as true of those who feel "out of harmony" with their surroundings as of those who are contented with them.

As a progressive and evolving being, man is where he is that he may learn that he may grow; and as he learns the spiritual lesson which any circumstance contains for him, it passes away and gives place to other circumstances.

Man is buffeted by circumstances so long as he believes himself to be the creature of outside conditions, but when he realizes that he is a creative power, and that he may command the hidden soil and seeds of his being out of which circumstances grow, he then becomes the rightful master of himself.

That circumstances grow out of thought every man knows who has for any length of time practised self-control and self-purification, for he will have noticed that the alteration in his circumstances has been in exact ratio with his altered mental condition. So true is this that when a man earnestly applies himself to remedy the defects in his character, and makes swift and marked progress, he passes rapidly through a succession of vicissitudes.

The soul attracts that which it secretly harbours; that which it loves, and also that which it fears; it reaches the height of its cherished aspirations; it falls to the level of its unchastened desires,—and circumstances are the means by which the soul receives its own.

Every thought-seed sown or allowed to fall into the mind, and to take root there, produces its own, blossoming sooner or later into act, and bearing its own fruitage of opportunity and circumstance. Good thoughts bear good fruit, bad thoughts bad fruit.

The outer world of circumstance shapes itself to the inner world of thought, and both pleasant and unpleasant external conditions are factors, which make for the ultimate good of the individual. As the reaper of his own harvest, man learns both by suffering and bliss.

Following the inmost desires, aspirations, thoughts, by which he allows himself to be dominated, (pursuing the will-o'-the-wisps of impure imaginings or steadfastly walking the highway of strong and high endeavour), a man at last arrives at their fruition and fulfilment in the outer conditions of his life. The laws of growth and adjustment everywhere obtains.

A man does not come to the almshouse or the jail by the tyranny of fate or circumstance, but by the pathway of grovelling thoughts and base desires. Nor does a pure-minded man fall suddenly into crime by stress of any mere external force; the criminal thought had long been secretly fostered in the heart, and the hour of opportunity revealed its gathered power. Circumstance does not make the man; it reveals him to himself No such conditions can exist as descending into vice and its attendant sufferings apart from vicious inclinations, or ascending into virtue and its pure happiness without the continued cultivation of virtuous aspirations; and man, therefore, as the lord and master of thought, is the maker of himself the shaper and author of environment. Even at birth the soul comes to its own and through every step of its earthly pilgrimage it attracts those combinations of conditions which reveal itself, which are the reflections of its own purity and, impurity, its strength and weakness.

Men do not attract that which they *want,* but that which they *are.* Their whims, fancies, and ambitions are thwarted at every step, but their inmost thoughts and desires are fed with their own food, be it foul or clean. The "divinity that shapes our ends"[5] is in ourselves; it is our very self. Only himself manacles man: thought and action are the gaolers of Fate—they imprison, being base; they are also the angels of Freedom—they liberate, being noble. Not what he wishes and prays for does a man get, but what he justly earns. His wishes and prayers are only gratified and answered when they harmonize with his thoughts and actions.

In the light of this truth, what, then, is the meaning of "fighting against circumstances?" It means that a man is continually revolting against an *effect* without, while all the time he is nourishing and preserving its *cause* in his heart.

[5] A subtle inversion of Shakespeare's *Hamlet* (Act V, Sc. II): *"There's a divinity that shapes our ends, rough-hew them how we will."* Allen relocates the divine from providence to the self.

That cause may take the form of a conscious vice or an unconscious weakness; but whatever it is, it stubbornly retards the efforts of its possessor, and thus calls aloud for remedy.

Men are anxious to improve their circumstances, but are unwilling to improve themselves; they therefore remain bound. The man who does not shrink from self-crucifixion can never fail to accomplish the object upon which his heart is set. This is as true of earthly as of heavenly things. Even the man whose sole object is to acquire wealth must be prepared to make great personal sacrifices before he can accomplish his object; and how much more so he who would realize a strong and well-poised life?

Here is a man who is wretchedly poor. He is extremely anxious that his surroundings and home comforts should be improved, yet all the time he shirks his work, and considers he is justified in trying to deceive his employer on the ground of the insufficiency of his wages. Such a man does not understand the simplest rudiments of those principles which are the basis of true prosperity, and is not only totally unfitted to rise out of his wretchedness, but is actually attracting to himself a still deeper wretchedness by dwelling in, and acting out, indolent, deceptive, and unmanly thoughts.

Here is a rich man who is the victim of a painful and persistent disease as the result of gluttony. He is willing to give large sums of money to get rid of it, but he will not sacrifice his gluttonous desires. He wants to gratify his taste for rich and unnatural viands and have his health as well. Such a man is totally unfit to have health, because he has not yet learned the first principles of a healthy life.

Here is an employer of labour who adopts crooked measures to avoid paying the regulation wage, and, in the hope of making larger profits, reduces the wages of his workpeople. Such a man is altogether unfitted for prosperity, and when he finds himself bankrupt, both as regards reputation and riches, he blames circumstances, not knowing that he is the sole author of his condition.

I have introduced these three cases merely as illustrative of the truth that man is the causer (though nearly always is unconsciously) of his circumstances, and that, whilst aiming at a good end, he is continually frustrating its accomplishment by encouraging thoughts and desires which cannot possibly harmonize with that end. Such cases could be multiplied and varied almost indefinitely, but this is not necessary, as the reader can, if he so resolves, trace the action of the laws of thought in his own mind and life, and until this is done, mere external facts cannot serve as a ground of reasoning.

Circumstances, however, are so complicated, thought is so deeply rooted, and the conditions of happiness vary so, vastly with individuals, that a man's entire soul-condition (although it may be known to himself) cannot be judged by another from the external aspect of his life alone. A man may be honest in certain directions, yet suffer privations; a man may be dishonest in certain directions, yet acquire wealth; but the conclusion usually formed that the one man fails *because of his particular honesty,* and that the other *prospers because of his particular dishonesty,* is the result of a superficial judgment, which assumes that the dishonest man is almost totally corrupt, and the honest man almost entirely virtuous. In the light of a deeper knowledge and wider experience such judgment is found to be erroneous. The dishonest man may have some admirable virtues, which the other does, not possess; and the honest man obnoxious vices which are absent in the other. The honest man reaps the good results of his honest thoughts and acts; he also brings upon himself the sufferings, which his vices produce. The dishonest man likewise garners his own suffering and happiness.

It is pleasing to human vanity to believe that one suffers because of one's virtue; but not until a man has extirpated every sickly, bitter, and impure thought from his mind, and washed every sinful stain from his soul, can he be in a position to know and declare that his sufferings are the result of his good, and not of his bad qualities; and on the way to, yet long before he has reached, that supreme perfection, he will have found, working in his mind and life, the Great Law which is absolutely just, and which cannot, therefore, give good for evil, evil for good. Possessed of such knowledge, he will then know, looking back upon his past ignorance and blindness, that his life is, and always was, justly ordered, and that all his past experiences, good and bad, were the equitable outworking of his evolving, yet unevolved self.

Good thoughts and actions can never produce bad results; bad thoughts and actions can never produce good results. This is but saying that nothing can come from corn but corn, nothing from nettles but nettles. Men understand this law in the natural world, and work with it; but few understand it in the mental and moral world (though its operation there is just as simple and undeviating), and they, therefore, do not co-operate with it.

Suffering is *always* the effect of wrong thought in some direction. It is an indication that the individual is out of harmony with himself, with the Law of his being. The sole and supreme use of suffering is to purify, to burn out all that is useless and impure. Suffering ceases for him who is pure. There could be no object in burning gold after the dross had been removed, and a perfectly pure and enlightened being could not suffer.

The circumstances, which a man encounters with suffering, are the result of his own mental in harmony. The circumstances, which a man encounters with blessedness, are the result of his own mental harmony. Blessedness, not material possessions, is the measure of right thought; wretchedness, not lack of material possessions, is the measure of wrong thought. A man may be cursed and rich; he may be blessed and poor. Blessedness and riches are only joined together when the riches are rightly and wisely used; and the poor man only descends into wretchedness when he regards his lot as a burden unjustly imposed.

Indigence and indulgence are the two extremes of wretchedness. They are both equally unnatural and the result of mental disorder. A man is not rightly conditioned until he is a happy, healthy, and prosperous being; and happiness, health, and prosperity are the result of a harmonious adjustment of the inner with the outer, of the man with his surroundings.

A man only begins to be a man when he ceases to whine and revile, and commences to search for the hidden justice which regulates his life. And as he adapts his mind to that regulating factor, he ceases to accuse others as the cause of his condition, and builds himself up in strong and noble thoughts; ceases to kick against circumstances, but begins to *use* them as aids to his more rapid progress, and as a means of discovering the hidden powers and possibilities within himself.

Law, not confusion, is the dominating principle in the universe; justice, not injustice, is the soul and substance of life; and righteousness, not corruption, is the moulding and moving force in the spiritual government of the world. This being so, man has but to right himself to find that the universe is right; and during the process of putting himself right he will find that as he alters his thoughts towards things and other people, things and other people will alter towards him.

The proof of this truth is in every person, and it therefore admits of easy investigation by systematic introspection and self-analysis. Let a man radically alter his thoughts, and he will be astonished at the rapid transformation it will effect in the material conditions of his life. Men imagine that thought can be kept secret, but it cannot; it rapidly crystallizes into habit, and habit solidifies into circumstance. Bestial thoughts crystallize into habits of drunkenness and sensuality, which solidify into circumstances of destitution and disease: impure thoughts of every kind crystallize into enervating and confusing habits, which solidify into distracting and adverse circumstances: thoughts of fear, doubt, and indecision crystallize into weak, unmanly, and irresolute habits, which solidify into circumstances of failure, indigence, and slavish dependence: lazy thoughts crystallize into habits of uncleanliness and dishonesty, which solidify into circumstances of foulness and beggary: hateful and condemnatory thoughts crystallize into habits of accusation and violence, which solidify into circumstances of injury and persecution: selfish thoughts of all kinds crystallize into habits of self-seeking, which solidify into circumstances more or less distressing. On the other hand, beautiful thoughts of all kinds crystallize into habits of grace and kindliness, which solidify into genial and sunny circumstances: pure thoughts crystallize into habits of temperance and self-control, which solidify into circumstances of repose and peace: thoughts of courage, self-reliance, and decision crystallize into manly habits, which solidify into circumstances of success, plenty, and freedom: energetic thoughts crystallize into habits of cleanliness and industry, which solidify into circumstances of pleasantness: gentle and forgiving thoughts crystallize into habits of gentleness, which solidify into protective and preservative circumstances: loving and unselfish thoughts crystallize into habits of self-forgetfulness for others, which solidify into circumstances of sure and abiding prosperity and true riches.

A particular train of thought persisted in, be it good or bad, cannot fail to produce its results on the character and circumstances. A man cannot *directly* choose his circumstances, but he can choose his thoughts, and so indirectly, yet surely, shape his circumstances.

Nature helps every man to the gratification of the thoughts, which he most encourages, and opportunities are presented which will most speedily bring to the surface both the good and evil thoughts.

Let a man cease from his sinful thoughts, and all the world will soften towards him, and be ready to help him; let him put away his weakly and sickly thoughts, and lo, opportunities will spring up on every hand to aid his strong resolves; let him encourage good thoughts, and no hard fate shall bind him down to wretchedness and shame. The world is your kaleidoscope, and the varying combinations of colours, which at every succeeding moment it presents to you are the exquisitely adjusted pictures of your ever-moving thoughts.

"So You will be what you will to be;
Let failure find its false content
In that poor word, 'environment,'
But spirit scorns it, and is free.

"It masters time, it conquers space;
It cowes that boastful trickster, Chance,
And bids the tyrant Circumstance
Uncrown, and fill a servant's place.
"The human Will, that force unseen,
The offspring of a deathless Soul,
Can hew a way to any goal,
Though walls of granite intervene.
"Be not impatient in delays
But wait as one who understands;
When spirit rises and commands
The gods are ready to obey."[6]

[6] This poem is often attributed to Ella Wheeler Wilcox, though Allen includes it without citation. The verse reflects the central tenets of will-power philosophy popular in late-19th century American optimism and New Thought writing.

EFFECT OF THOUGHT ON

HEALTH

AND

THE BODY

THE body is the servant of the mind.[7] It obeys the operations of the mind, whether they be deliberately chosen or automatically expressed. At the bidding of unlawful thoughts the body sinks rapidly into disease and decay; at the command of glad and beautiful thoughts it becomes clothed with youthfulness and beauty.

Disease and health, like circumstances, are rooted in thought. Sickly thoughts will express themselves through a sickly body. Thoughts of fear have been known to kill a man as speedily as a bullet, and they are continually killing thousands of people just as surely though less rapidly. The people who live in fear of disease are the people who get it. Anxiety quickly demoralizes the whole body, and

[7] This reflects a long philosophical tradition, from Plato to Descartes to New Thought, in which the mind is treated as superior or governing. Allen aligns with idealism, in contrast to the materialist model dominant in late 19th-century medicine.

lays it open to the entrance of disease; while impure thoughts,[8] even if not physically indulged, will soon shatter the nervous system.

Strong, pure, and happy thoughts build up the body in vigour and grace. The body is a delicate and plastic instrument, which responds readily to the thoughts by which it is impressed, and habits of thought will produce their own effects, good or bad, upon it.

Men will continue to have impure and poisoned blood, so long as they propagate unclean thoughts. Out of a clean heart comes a clean life and a clean body. Out of a defiled mind proceeds a defiled life and a corrupt body. Thought is the fount of action, life, and manifestation; make the fountain pure, and all will be pure.

Change of diet will not help a man who will not change his thoughts. When a man makes his thoughts pure, he no longer desires impure food.

Clean thoughts make clean habits. The so-called saint who does not wash his body is not a saint. He who has strengthened and purified his thoughts does not need to consider the malevolent microbe.

[8] 19th-century morality often equated physical degeneration with moral failing. Allen's phrasing echoes Victorian concerns with "nervous collapse" and the rising diagnosis of "neurasthenia," commonly associated with sexual excess or anxiety.

If you would protect your body, guard your mind. If you would renew your body, beautify your mind. Thoughts of malice, envy, disappointment, despondency, rob the body of its health and grace. A sour face does not come by chance; it is made by sour thoughts. Wrinkles that mar are drawn by folly, passion, and pride.

I know a woman of ninety-six who has the bright, innocent face of a girl. I know a man well under middle age whose face is drawn into inharmonious contours. The one is the result of a sweet and sunny disposition; the other is the outcome of passion and discontent.

As you cannot have a sweet and wholesome abode unless you admit the air and sunshine freely into your rooms, so a strong body and a bright, happy, or serene countenance can only result from the free admittance into the mind of thoughts of joy and goodwill and serenity.

On the faces of the aged there are wrinkles made by sympathy, others by strong and pure thought, and others are carved by passion: who cannot distinguish them? With those who have lived righteously, age is calm, peaceful, and softly mellowed, like the setting sun. I have recently seen a philosopher on his deathbed. He was not old except in years. He died as sweetly and peacefully as he had lived.

There is no physician like cheerful thought for dissipating the ills of the body; there is no comforter to compare with goodwill for dispersing the shadows of grief and sorrow. To live continually in thoughts of ill will, cynicism, suspicion, and envy, is to be confined in a self made prison-hole. But to think well of all, to be cheerful with all, to patiently learn to find the good in all—such unselfish thoughts are the very portals of heaven; and to dwell day by day in thoughts of peace toward every creature will bring abounding peace to their possessor.

THOUGHT

AND

PURPOSE

UNTIL thought is linked with purpose there is no intelligent accomplishment. With the majority the bark of thought is allowed to "drift" upon the ocean of life. Aimlessness is a vice, and such drifting must not continue for him who would steer clear of catastrophe and destruction.

They who have no central purpose in their life fall an easy prey to petty worries, fears, troubles, and self-pityings, all of which are indications of weakness, which lead, just as surely as deliberately planned sins (though by a different route), to failure, unhappiness, and loss, for weakness cannot persist in a power evolving universe.

A man should conceive of a legitimate purpose in his heart, and set out to accomplish it. He should make this purpose the centralizing point of his thoughts. It may take the form of a spiritual ideal, or it may be a worldly object, according to his nature at the time being; but whichever it is, he should steadily focus his thought-forces upon the object, which he has set before him. He should make this purpose his supreme duty, and should devote himself to its attainment, not allowing his thoughts to wander away into ephemeral fancies, longings, and imaginings. This is the royal road to self-control and true concentration of thought. Even if he fails again and again to accomplish his purpose (as he necessarily must until weakness is overcome), the *strength of character gained* will be the measure of *his true* success, and this will form a new starting-point for future power and triumph.

Those who are not prepared for the apprehension of a *great* purpose should fix the thoughts upon the faultless performance of their duty, no matter how insignificant their task may appear. Only in this way can the thoughts be gathered and focussed, and resolution and energy be developed, which being done, there is nothing which may not be accomplished.

The weakest soul, knowing its own weakness, and believing this truth *that strength can only be developed by effort and practice,* will, thus believing, at once begin to exert itself, and, adding effort to effort, patience to patience, and strength to strength, will never cease to develop, and will at last grow divinely strong.

As the physically weak man can make himself strong by careful and patient training, so the man of weak thoughts can make them strong by exercising himself in right thinking.

To put away aimlessness and weakness, and to begin to think with purpose, is to enter the ranks of those strong ones who only recognize failure as one of the pathways to attainment; who make all conditions serve them, and who think strongly, attempt fearlessly, and accomplish masterfully.

Having conceived of his purpose, a man should mentally mark out a *straight* pathway to its achievement, looking neither to the right nor the left. Doubts and fears should be rigorously excluded; they are disintegrating elements, which break up the straight line of effort, rendering it crooked, ineffectual, useless. Thoughts of doubt and fear[9] never accomplished anything, and never can. They always lead to failure. Purpose, energy, power to do, and all strong thoughts cease when doubt and fear creep in.

The will to do springs from the knowledge[10] that we *can* do. Doubt and fear are the great enemies of knowledge, and he who encourages them, who does not slay them, thwarts himself at every step.

[9] A classic example of heroic moral philosophy, reminiscent of Stoicism, Christian asceticism, and Hindu *karma yoga*, where internal mastery precedes any outward success.

[10] This anticipates Bandura's theory of self-efficacy (1977), which argues that belief in one's capacity to act is essential for motivation and performance. Allen intuited this long before it was framed in psychological terms.

He who has conquered doubt and fear has conquered failure. His every thought is allied with power, and all difficulties are bravely met and wisely overcome. His purposes are seasonably planted, and they bloom and bring forth fruit, which does not fall prematurely to the ground.

Thought allied fearlessly to purpose becomes creative force: he who *knows* this is ready to become something higher and stronger than a mere bundle of wavering thoughts and fluctuating sensations; he who *does* this has become the conscious and intelligent wielder of his mental powers.

THE THOUGHT-FACTOR
IN
ACHIEVEMENT

ALL that a man achieves and all that he fails to achieve is the direct result of his own thoughts. In a justly ordered universe, where loss of equipoise would mean total destruction, individual responsibility must be absolute. A man's weakness and strength, purity and impurity, are his own, and not another man's; they are brought about by himself, and not by another; and they can only be altered by himself, never by another. His condition is also his own, and not another man's. His suffering and his happiness are evolved from within. As he thinks, so he is; as he continues to think, so he remains.

A strong man cannot help a weaker unless that weaker is *willing* to be helped, and even then the weak man must become strong of himself; he must, by his own efforts, develop the strength which he admires in another. None but himself can alter his condition.

It has been usual for men to think and to say, "Many men are slaves because one is an oppressor; let us hate the oppressor." Now, however, there is amongst an increasing few a tendency to reverse this judgment, and to say, "One man is an oppressor because many are slaves; let us despise the slaves."

The truth is that oppressor and slave are co-operators in ignorance, and, while seeming to afflict each other, are in reality afflicting themselves. A perfect Knowledge perceives the action of law in the weakness of the oppressed and the misapplied power of the oppressor; a perfect Love, seeing the suffering, which both states entail, condemns neither; a perfect Compassion embraces both oppressor and oppressed.

He who has conquered weakness, and has put away all selfish thoughts, belongs neither to oppressor nor oppressed. He is free.

A man can only rise, conquer, and achieve by lifting up his thoughts. He can only remain weak, and abject, and miserable by refusing to lift up his thoughts.

Before a man can achieve anything, even in worldly things, he must lift his thoughts above slavish animal indulgence. He may not, in order to succeed, give up all animality and selfishness, by any means; but a portion of it must, at least, be sacrificed. A man whose first thought is bestial indulgence could neither think clearly nor plan methodically; he could not find and develop his latent resources, and would fail in any undertaking. Not having commenced to manfully control his thoughts, he is not in a position to control affairs and to adopt serious responsibilities. He is not fit to act independently and stand alone. But he is limited only by the thoughts, which he chooses.

There can be no progress, no achievement without sacrifice, and a man's worldly success will be in the measure that he sacrifices his confused animal thoughts, and fixes his mind on the development of his plans, and the strengthening of his resolution and self-reliance. And the higher he lifts his thoughts, the more manly, upright, and righteous he becomes, the greater will be his success, the more blessed and enduring will be his achievements.

The universe does not favour the greedy, the dishonest, the vicious, although on the mere surface it may sometimes appear to do so; it helps the honest, the magnanimous, the virtuous. All the great Teachers of the ages have declared this in varying forms, and to prove and know it a man has but to persist in making himself more and more virtuous by lifting up his thoughts.

Intellectual achievements are the result of thought consecrated to the search for knowledge, or for the beautiful and true in life and nature. Such achievements may be sometimes connected with vanity and ambition, but they are not the outcome of those characteristics; they are the natural outgrowth of long and arduous effort, and of pure and unselfish thoughts.

Spiritual achievements are the consummation of holy aspirations. He who lives constantly in the conception of noble and lofty thoughts, who dwells upon all that is pure and unselfish, will, as surely as the sun reaches its zenith and the moon its full, become wise and noble in character, and rise into a position of influence and blessedness.

Achievement, of whatever kind, is the crown of effort, the diadem of thought. By the aid of self-control, resolution, purity, righteousness, and well-directed thought a man ascends; by the aid of animality, indolence, impurity, corruption, and confusion of thought a man descends.

A man may rise to high success in the world, and even to lofty altitudes in the spiritual realm, and again descend into weakness and wretchedness by allowing arrogant, selfish, and corrupt thoughts to take possession of him.

Victories attained by right thought can only be maintained by watchfulness. Many give way when success is assured, and rapidly fall back into failure.

All achievements, whether in the business, intellectual, or spiritual world, are the result of definitely directed thought, are governed by the same law and are of the same method; the only difference lies in *the object of attainment.*

He who would accomplish little must sacrifice little; he who would achieve much must sacrifice much; he who would attain highly must sacrifice greatly.

Dream lofty dreams, and as you dream,

so shall you become.

—James Allen.

VISIONS AND IDEALS

THE dreamers are the saviours of the world. As the visible world is sustained by the invisible[11], so men, through all their trials and sins and sordid vocations, are nourished by the beautiful visions of their solitary dreamers. Humanity cannot forget its dreamers; it cannot let their ideals fade and die; it lives in them; it knows them as the *realities* which it shall one day see and know.

Composer, sculptor, painter, poet, prophet, sage, these are the makers of the after-world, the architects of

[11] A metaphysical claim found in Plato's theory of forms, Christian mysticism, and Eastern philosophy (e.g., the *unmanifest* in Vedanta). Allen implies that outer reality is shaped by inner ideals.

heaven. The world is beautiful because they have lived; without them, labouring humanity would perish.

He who cherishes a beautiful vision, a lofty ideal in his heart, will one day realize it. Columbus cherished a vision of another world, and he discovered it; Copernicus fostered the vision of a multiplicity of worlds and a wider universe, and he revealed it; Buddha beheld the vision of a spiritual world of stainless beauty and perfect peace, and he entered into it.

Cherish your visions; cherish your ideals; cherish the music that stirs in your heart, the beauty that forms in your mind, the loveliness that drapes your purest thoughts, for out of them will grow all delightful conditions, all, heavenly environment; of these, if you but remain true to them, your world will at last be built.

To desire is to obtain; to aspire is to, achieve. Shall man's basest desires receive the fullest measure of gratification, and his purest aspirations starve for lack of sustenance? Such is not the Law: such a condition of things can never obtain: "ask and receive."[12]

[12] Direct reference to Matthew 7:7, a verse central to Christian faith and often quoted in New Thought: *"Ask, and it shall be given you; seek, and ye shall find..."*

Dream lofty dreams[13], and as you dream, so shall you become. Your Vision is the promise of what you shall one day be; your Ideal is the prophecy of what you shall at last unveil.

The greatest achievement was at first and for a time a dream. The oak sleeps in the acorn; the bird waits in the egg; and in the highest vision of the soul a waking angel stirs. Dreams are the seedlings of realities.

Your circumstances may be uncongenial, but they shall not long remain so if you but perceive an Ideal and strive to reach it. You cannot travel *within*and stand still *without.* Here is a youth hard pressed by poverty and labour; confined long hours in an unhealthy workshop; unschooled, and lacking all the arts of refinement. But he dreams of better things; he thinks of intelligence, of refinement, of grace and beauty. He conceives of, mentally builds up, an ideal condition of life; the vision of a wider liberty and a larger scope takes possession of him; unrest urges him to action, and he utilizes all his spare time and means, small though they are, to the development of his latent powers and resources. Very soon so altered has his mind become that the workshop can no longer hold him. It has become so out of harmony with his mentality that

[13] This mirrors Proverbs 29:18 ("Where there is no vision, the people perish") and reflects Platonic idealism, where the soul contains pre-existent forms that it seeks to manifest in life.

it falls out of his life as a garment is cast aside, and, with the growth of opportunities, which fit the scope of his expanding powers, he passes out of it forever. Years later we see this youth as a full-grown man. We find him a master of certain forces of the mind, which he wields with worldwide influence and almost unequalled power. In his hands he holds the cords of gigantic responsibilities; he speaks, and lo, lives are changed; men and women hang upon his words and remould their characters, and, sunlike, he becomes the fixed and luminous centre round which innumerable destinies revolve. He has realized the Vision of his youth. He has become one with his Ideal.

And you, too, youthful reader, will realize the Vision (not the idle wish) of your heart, be it base or beautiful, or a mixture of both, for you will always gravitate toward that which you, secretly, most love. Into your hands will be placed the exact results of your own thoughts; you will receive that which you earn; no more, no less. Whatever your present environment may be, you will fall, remain, or rise with your thoughts, your Vision, your Ideal. You will become as small as your controlling desire; as great as your dominant aspiration: in the beautiful words of Stanton Kirkham Davis,[14] "You may be keeping

[14] Davis (1868–1945) was a philosopher and poet associated with American individualism and spiritual optimism. The passage is from *The Ministry*

accounts, and presently you shall walk out of the door that for so long has seemed to you the barrier of your ideals, and shall find yourself before an audience—the pen still behind your ear, the ink stains on your fingers and then and there shall pour out the torrent of your inspiration. You may be driving sheep, and you shall wander to the city-bucolic and open-mouthed; shall wander under the intrepid guidance of the spirit into the studio of the master, and after a time he shall say, 'I have nothing more to teach you.' And now you have become the master, who did so recently dream of great things while driving sheep. You shall lay down the saw and the plane to take upon yourself the regeneration of the world."

The thoughtless, the ignorant, and the indolent, seeing only the apparent effects of things and not the things themselves, talk of luck, of fortune, and chance. Seeing a man grow rich, they say, "How lucky he is!" Observing another become intellectual, they exclaim, "How highly favoured he is!" And noting the saintly character and wide influence of another, they remark, "How chance aids him at every turn!" They do not see the trials and failures and struggles which these men have voluntarily encountered in order to gain their experience; have no

of Beauty (1907). Allen quotes it as a testimony to latent greatness emerging through discipline and inspiration.

knowledge of the sacrifices they have made, of the undaunted efforts they have put forth, of the faith they have exercised, that they might overcome the apparently insurmountable, and realize the Vision of their heart. They do not know the darkness and the heartaches; they only see the light and joy, and call it "luck". They do not see the long and arduous journey, but only behold the pleasant goal, and call it "good fortune," do not understand the process, but only perceive the result, and call it chance.

In all human affairs there are *efforts,* and there are *results,* and the strength of the effort is the measure of the result. Chance is not. Gifts, powers, material, intellectual, and spiritual possessions are the fruits of effort; they are thoughts completed, objects accomplished, visions realized.

The Vision that you glorify in your mind, the Ideal that you enthrone in your heart—this you will build your life by, this you will become.

SERENITY

CALMNESS of mind is one of the beautiful jewels of wisdom. It is the result of long and patient effort in self-control. Its presence is an indication of ripened experience, and of a more than ordinary knowledge of the laws and operations of thought.

A man becomes calm in the measure that he understands himself as a thought evolved being, for such knowledge necessitates the understanding of others as the result of thought, and as he develops a right understanding[15], and sees more and more clearly the internal relations of things by the action of cause and effect he ceases to fuss and fume and worry and grieve, and remains poised, steadfast, serene.

The calm man, having learned how to govern himself, knows how to adapt himself to others; and they, in turn, reverence his spiritual strength, and feel that they can learn of him and rely upon him. The more tranquil a man

[15] The idea of *right understanding* is a direct echo of the Buddhist Noble Eightfold Path (*sammā-diṭṭhi*), in which it represents the foundation of spiritual progress.

becomes, the greater is his success, his influence, his power for good. Even the ordinary trader will find his business prosperity increase as he develops a greater self-control and equanimity, for people will always prefer to deal with a man whose demeanour is strongly equable.

The strong, calm man is always loved and revered. He is like a shade-giving tree in a thirsty land, or a sheltering rock in a storm. "Who does not love a tranquil heart, a sweet-tempered, balanced life? It does not matter whether it rains or shines, or what changes come to those possessing these blessings, for they are always sweet, serene, and calm. That exquisite poise of character, which we call serenity is the last lesson of culture, the fruitage of the soul. It is precious as wisdom, more to be desired than gold—yea, than even fine gold. How insignificant mere money seeking looks in comparison with a serene life—a life that dwells in the ocean of Truth, beneath the waves, beyond the reach of tempests, in the Eternal Calm!

"How many people we know who sour their lives, who ruin all that is sweet and beautiful by explosive tempers, who destroy their poise of character, and make bad blood! It is a question whether the great majority of people do not ruin their lives and mar their happiness by lack of self-control. How few people we meet in life who are well balanced, who have that exquisite poise which is characteristic of the finished character!

Yes, humanity surges with uncontrolled passion, is tumultuous with ungoverned grief, is blown about by anxiety and doubt only the wise man, only he whose thoughts are controlled and purified, makes the winds and the storms of the soul obey him.

Tempest-tossed souls, wherever ye may be, under whatsoever conditions ye may live, know this in the ocean of life the isles of Blessedness are smiling, and the sunny shore of your ideal awaits your coming. Keep your hand firmly upon the helm of thought. In the bark of your soul reclines the commanding Master;[16] He does but sleep: wake Him. Self-control is strength; Right Thought is mastery; Calmness is power. Say unto your heart, "Peace, be still!"

[16] This mystical image may allude to Christ sleeping in the boat (cf. Mark 4:39), where the disciples awaken Him during a storm. The phrase "Peace, be still!" is a direct reference to that Gospel story, used metaphorically for inner awakening and mastery.

James Allen's *As a Man Thinketh* (1903): Historical Context and Long-Term Relevance

SETTING THE STAGE: BRITAIN IN 1903 AND THE NEW THOUGHT MOVEMENT

In the year 1903, Edwardian Britain stood at the cusp of modernity while still echoing Victorian values. It was a time of rapid social change in the wake of the Industrial Revolution – factories had transformed cities, a new urban working class had emerged, and progressive movements for labor rights and education were underway. Amid these post-industrial changes, there remained a strong cultural emphasis on moral character and self-improvement, a legacy of the Victorian era. Victorian morality famously extolled personal virtues like hard work, perseverance, thrift, and self-reliance as the keys to bettering one's lot. The best-selling self-help book of the mid-19th century, Samuel Smiles's *Self-Help* (1859), had epitomized this ethic by trumpeting *"the virtues of hard work, perseverance and commitment at an individual level,"* shifting focus from collective circumstances to personal accountability. By the turn of the 20th century, this outlook – that *character* and personal effort determine one's destiny – was deeply ingrained in mainstream British thought.

At the same time, new currents of thought were flowing across the Atlantic. The New Thought movement, which had originated in late 19th-century America, was gaining adherents internationally, including in Britain. New Thought was a metaphysical and spiritual movement premised on the bold idea that thoughts could directly affect reality – that right thinking could heal, prosper, and transform one's life. Pioneered by figures like Phineas P. Quimby in the U.S., New Thought teachings emphasized the *"power of positive thinking"*, the use of affirmations, and mental healing techniques. By 1900–1903, these ideas had spread through lectures, journals, and books not only in America but also in Britain and beyond. Many followers of New Thought considered themselves Christian, blending religious faith with mind-healing principles. This was an era when people were seeking practical spirituality – a way to reconcile the scientific progress of the age with enduring spiritual yearnings. In churches and meeting halls, a "mind-cure" culture was arising, encouraging individuals to harness thought and mental discipline to improve their health and circumstances.

It was in this fertile environment – a Britain straddling its traditional moral code and new metaphysical ideas – that James Allen wrote and published *As a Man Thinketh.* Allen, an Englishman from a working-class background, absorbed both the Victorian faith in self-help and the New Thought belief in mind power. When he brought out this slim volume in 1903, he was speaking to the concerns of his time: how an ordinary person might rise above hardship and shape their own destiny through the power of thought. The book's very title, *As a Man Thinketh*, comes from the Bible (Proverbs 23:7: "As a man thinketh in his heart, so is he"), immediately rooting it in a familiar Christian context. Yet the message Allen delivered was in many ways novel for its day. He suggested that the mind is the ultimate shaper of character and circumstance, writing that *"in his own thought-world, each man holds the key to every condition, good or bad, that enters into his life"*, and by mastering thoughts one can *"remake his life, and transform his circumstances"*. Such ideas resonated with the optimistic spirit of the early 20th century, even as they gently challenged the era's more conventional notions of success being determined by external fate or social station.

Christian, Classical, and Literary Influences on Allen

James Allen did not invent his philosophy in a vacuum. *As a Man Thinketh* emerged from a rich tapestry of intellectual and cultural influences that shaped Allen's worldview. Foremost among these was Christianity. Allen was raised in an England where the Bible was a moral compass for society, and his writings are imbued with biblical language and concepts. The very premise that *thought precedes action and character* reflects a biblical moral order: as one sows, so shall one reap. Allen's emphasis on *virtue, purity, and faith* owes much to the Christian tradition of self-examination and moral uplift. His book frequently invokes ideals of *"wisdom," "blessedness,"* and *"divine perfection,"* echoing Christian ethics even as it presents them in a practical, secular tone. In one of his later writings, Allen's wife Lily noted that his literary mission was essentially spiritual – he *"wrote when he had a message,"* only after living out and proving his principles in practice. This reflects a profoundly Christian ethos of integrity: truth must be lived, not just preached.

At the same time, Allen drew on classical Stoicism and other ancient philosophies that stress mastery over one's own mind. Though he seldom quoted Stoic authors explicitly, the parallels are striking. The Roman emperor-philosopher Marcus Aurelius once wrote, *"The soul becomes dyed with the color of its thoughts,"* encapsulating the Stoic belief that our mental impressions shape our inner life. Allen's entire essay builds on this premise. His assertion that *"a man is literally what he thinks, his character being the complete sum of all his thoughts"* could have come from Epictetus or Seneca as easily as from a New Testament epistle. The Stoics taught self-control, virtue, and inner tranquility in the face of life's vicissitudes – themes that Allen passionately reiterates. For example, Allen's idea that calmness is power and that serenity comes from right thinking aligns with Stoic teachings about equanimity. We know that late-Victorian educators often introduced students to the classics; it is likely Allen encountered Stoic ideas through cultural osmosis if not formal study. His work serves as a bridge between ancient wisdom and modern self-help, reframing timeless advice on governing one's thoughts in a simple, relatable way for the everyman.

Allen was also indebted to the 19th-century self-help literature that preceded him. As mentioned, Samuel Smiles's *Self-Help* was a publishing phenomenon in England – by some accounts second only to the Bible in popularity in its time. Smiles and his Victorian contemporaries promoted the gospel of personal improvement: biographies of great men, aphorisms about diligence and character, and a conviction that anyone could rise from humble origins through effort and integrity. Allen, born in 1864 to a struggling family in Leicester, was very much a product of this culture. In fact, his own life story mirrored a classic Victorian *"rags-to-respectability"* arc. As a teenager, Allen had to leave school and work in factory offices after his father's tragic death, scratching out a living in industrial England. He educated himself in his spare time. This background gave Allen a deep empathy for strivers of modest means and a belief – typical of Victorian liberalism – that character was the decisive factor in one's fate. He thus extolled habits like industry, honesty, and focused ambition, much as Smiles had done a generation earlier. But Allen's innovation was to add a metaphysical dimension: where a Victorian moralist might say "work hard and be virtuous," Allen would add "because your thoughts *create* your reality." In this way, *As a Man Thinketh* both upheld Victorian ideals and transcended them, injecting the power of mind into the established narrative of self-help.

Less obvious, but equally important, were Allen's encounters with Eastern and humanistic philosophies. By the early 1900s, translations of Buddhist and Hindu texts were available in English and had sparked interest among Western spiritual seekers. James Allen proved to be an avid seeker. As one historian notes, Allen *"drank deeply from Eastern spirituality (he was among the first Westerners to popularize principles of Buddhism), [from] American motivational and mind-power philosophy, and the rock-ribbed moralism of Victorian England*[17]. Indeed, Allen's writings stress *mindfulness* and the cultivation of inner peace in a way that resonates with Buddhism. His call for complete responsibility over one's own thoughts parallels the Buddha's teaching that *"All that we are is the result of what we have thought."* Moreover, Allen's gentle, almost ascetic personal life – he eventually withdrew to a quiet village in Ilfracombe to write, living simply with his wife – was reminiscent of Tolstoyan and Buddhist ideals. Contemporary accounts describe Allen as a kind of mystic of everyday life. He eschewed fame and materialism, aiming instead to *"master all of the virtues"* and live in harmony with the law of love. Like the Russian novelist Tolstoy in his later years, Allen practiced voluntary simplicity – a life of few possessions, manual work (gardening and chores), and compassion toward all creatures (Allen was reportedly a vegetarian who would not harm even a mouse). This melding of East and West in Allen's influences gave *As a Man Thinketh* a unique universalist flavor. The book draws on Christian morality, Stoic self-discipline, and New Thought optimism, but also radiates a serene, almost Buddhist faith in the law of cause and effect in the moral universe.

[17] Horowitz, M. (2020, March 21). Working-class sage. *Medium.*

Within and Beyond Mainstream Thought of Its Time

When *As a Man Thinketh* was published, it both reflected and departed from the mainstream thought of its era. On one hand, Allen's core message would have sounded familiar and respectable to an early 20th-century reader steeped in Victorian and Christian teachings. His insistence on personal responsibility for one's condition – the idea that our "thoughts and character are one" – strongly echoed the Victorian moral maxim that individuals largely shape their own destiny through character and conduct. In a society that valued self-reliance, this was a reassuring affirmation that *the old virtues still mattered.* Allen's writing is earnest and exhortative, much like a sermon or a morality tract; he speaks of *honesty*, *purpose*, *goodness*, and *self-discipline* as the foundations of a well-lived life. Such language was very much in line with the moral mainstream of the time. Even the book's small, unadorned format (Allen called it "A pocket companion for thoughtful people" priced at one shilling) suggests he intended it for a broad audience, including working-class readers who were accustomed to pamphlets on self-improvement and Christian virtue.

Yet in other respects, Allen's philosophy stood a little *to the side* of early 20th-century mainstream thought – *almost quietly revolutionary*. Consider the prevailing intellectual currents of the day: the early 1900s were marked by growing faith in science, the influence of social Darwinism, and the onset of modern psychology. Many learned people were beginning to attribute human behavior to heredity, environment, or the subconscious, rather than individual will. Socialist ideas about class conditions and economic structures determining one's fate were also gaining ground in Edwardian Britain. In this context, Allen's declaration that thoughts are the supreme factor in shaping one's reality was a departure from the norm. He was, in effect, reasserting idealism in an age tilting toward material explanations. *As a Man Thinketh* posits an almost absolute inner freedom: regardless of one's external circumstances, one can think oneself into (or out of) virtuous character, health, and prosperity. This was not a common view among orthodox thinkers. Traditional Christianity, for example, emphasized human sinfulness and reliance on God's grace; Allen by contrast emphasizes human mental agency and *"divine"* potential within. Likewise, where social reformers of the time focused on external remedies for poverty and vice (better wages, housing, education), Allen unabashedly asserts that poverty or prosperity spring from a man's mindset above all – a notion some would have seen as too individualistic or even blaming the victim.

It is fair to say that James Allen occupied a middle ground between conventional morality and radical New Thought. He did not go as far as some New Thought writers who promised near-magical results (wealth or miraculous healing) purely from thought or faith. Allen's tone is more sober and ethical: thoughts must be aligned with duty and virtue to yield *"happy and beautiful issues"*, he maintained. This emphasis kept him within the comfort zone of many Christian readers. Still, by treating mind as the motor of fate, Allen subtly challenged the era's fatalism. His book suggested that the common man had more power than he realized – that each person is "the master gardener" of his soul, planting seeds of thought that bloom into destiny. In doing so, Allen's work departed from the class-bound thinking of his society (where it was often assumed one's station in life was fixed) and from the emerging scientific skepticism about metaphysical concepts. If mainstream academic opinion in 1903 largely ignored *As a Man Thinketh* (it was too folksy and mystical to attract scholarly notice), the book nevertheless found a receptive fringe audience. It circulated among spiritual seekers, temperance advocates, and self-improvement circles who were open to the blend of old-fashioned virtue and new-fangled mental science. Over time, what was once a fringe idea – the law of the mind as a literal force in life – would seep into popular culture, vindicating Allen's forward-looking stance. In the short run, however, *As a Man Thinketh* remained somewhat "out of place" in its era: a quietly prophetic text awaiting a future audience that could fully appreciate it.

FROM OBSCURITY TO INSPIRATION: THE BOOK'S RECEPTION AND LEGACY

James Allen published *As a Man Thinketh* with modest expectations. In fact, the book almost didn't see the light of day – Allen initially underestimated his own work. According to one account, he was actually dissatisfied with the manuscript, and it was his wife, Lily, who *"had to persuade him to publish it."* Allen failed to recognize that this concise essay, which so elegantly distilled his philosophy, would become his masterpiece. Upon its release in 1903, *As a Man Thinketh* did not make a grand splash. It found a small but steady readership, enough that Allen was encouraged to continue writing and even quit his day job to pursue a literary career. Still, during Allen's lifetime, he remained far from a household name. He received little fame or fortune; by all accounts, he lived simply and quietly, pleased more by the personal letters of thanks he got from readers than by any public recognition. One early 20th-century observer called Allen *"a literary mystery man"* – his books touched many lives, yet the author himself stayed almost unknown. He produced a remarkable stream of nearly 19 books in nine years, then died in 1912 at age 47, his work largely eulogized only in niche spiritual journals.

It was in the decades after his death that *As a Man Thinketh* steadily gained a *cult following* and then entered the mainstream of inspirational literature. The book benefited from being in the public domain (due to its age), which allowed it to be reprinted widely and cheaply. Throughout the mid-20th century, as the "positive thinking" movement surged, Allen's words found new life. By the 1920s, Western culture had increasingly embraced the idea of practical self-improvement undergirded by spiritual principles. Historians note that *"by the 1920s, spiritual self-help, promoted in books such as James Allen's As a Man Thinketh, led religious congregants to desire a 'usefulness' from their faith,"* fueling a rise in organizations that combined scientific psychology, self-help methods, and religious ideas.[18] In other words, ordinary churchgoers wanted techniques to improve their daily lives – prosperity, health, confidence – not just promises of heaven. Allen's little book, with its clear assurance that *"each man holds the key to every condition… in his own thought-world,"* fit perfectly into this trend. It became, as one writer put it, an *informal motto* for the burgeoning self-help movement. Motivational thinkers in America were especially influenced by it. For example, Napoleon Hill, author of *Think and Grow Rich* (1937), and Norman Vincent Peale, author of *The Power of Positive Thinking* (1952), are often cited as having drawn inspiration from James Allen's work. Hill's famous dictum, "What you think, so you become," is essentially an expansion of Allen's core premise. Indeed, Allen today is recognized as a pioneer whose shoulders many later self-help giants stood upon.

Over the twentieth century, *As a Man Thinketh* was mass-produced and globally disseminated, achieving a readership far beyond anything James Allen saw in his lifetime. Its reception evolved from quiet appreciation to almost scriptural status in the self-improvement canon. By the late 20th and early 21st centuries, the book had been translated into numerous languages and was being handed out in seminars, quoted in motivational speeches, and included in anthologies of great inspirational writings. Modern personal development gurus

[18] Horowitz, M. (2014, January). *One Simple Idea: How Positive Thinking Reshaped Modern Life* [Review of the book *One Simple Idea: How Positive Thinking Reshaped Modern Life*, by M. Horowitz]. *Library Journal*, 336, 24.

routinely praise its simplicity and timeless wisdom. While some contemporary readers might find the Edwardian prose a bit antiquated or the outlook naively optimistic, the consensus is that *As a Man Thinketh* captured a fundamental truth about human nature that transcends its time. The phrase *"as you think, so shall you be,"* popularized by Allen (and derived from biblical and classical sources), has entered the cultural lexicon as a shorthand for the power of mindset.

Crucially, Allen's work helped shape the genre of modern motivational literature. Many of the now-familiar tropes of self-help writing – the call to take personal responsibility, the assurance that changing one's thoughts can change one's life, the blend of ethical guidance with practical advice – were distilled in *As a Man Thinketh.* Later authors expanded on these ideas, applying them to wealth, relationships, leadership, and beyond, but the heart of it remains Allen's insight that *everything begins with a thought.* As one review of the positive-thinking movement notes, by mid-century the notion of harnessing thoughts had *"entered the mainstream"* of American life, influencing business, psychology, and even politics. We see this legacy in the success of countless books and programs that echo Allen's philosophy, from self-esteem curricula in schools to cognitive-behavioral techniques in therapy that teach people to reframe negative thinking.

More than 120 years after its publication, *As a Man Thinketh* continues to be rediscovered by new generations. Its longevity can be attributed to its brevity and depth – it is easily read in an afternoon, yet invites a lifetime of reflection. The book's narrative of empowerment – that each person, by mastering their inner world, can rise above external trials – remains deeply relevant in our modern era of uncertainty. If Allen's language belongs to 1903, his message certainly does not. In the end, *As a Man Thinketh* has proven to be both a product of its historical moment and a timeless beacon. Grounded in the bedrock of Victorian virtue and Christian wisdom, informed by New Thought and ancient philosophy, James Allen's little volume became a foundational text of personal development. Its journey from a quiet English printing to a worldwide inspirational classic illustrates a profound point in itself: the enduring power of an idea. As Allen wrote, *"men do not attract that which they want, but that which they are."* By helping readers *become* better, wiser, and more purposeful through the cultivation of thought, *As a Man Thinketh* earned a place as a cornerstone in the literature of self-mastery – a legacy still unfolding today.

James Allen: A Life Shaped by Thought

The story of James Allen, author of *As a Man Thinketh*, is as quietly remarkable as the philosophy he shared with the world—a life marked not by outward spectacle, but by the steady unfolding of inward conviction, resilience, and a rare dedication to the power of thought.

EARLY YEARS: ROOTS IN HARDSHIP AND HOPE

James Allen was born on November 28, 1864, in the industrial city of Leicester, England. His father, William, worked as a factory knitter, and his mother, Martha, tended to their modest home. The Allens were of humble means, but theirs was a household not lacking in affection or ambition. Like so many English families of the era, their lives were defined by the rhythms of labor and the aspirations that even poverty could not quell.

Young James's childhood, however, was marked by an event that would change the course of his life. In 1879, when James was just 15, his father set out for America, lured by stories of opportunity and work that could provide for the family's future. Tragedy intervened: not long after arriving in

New York, William Allen was robbed and murdered—a crime that left the family bereft, both emotionally and financially. The loss plunged James and his family into immediate hardship. Forced to leave school, James began work in a series of industrial and clerical jobs, first as a stationer's assistant, then as a private secretary, and later as a journalist's clerk. His formal education may have ended, but his real education was just beginning.

SELF-EDUCATION AND SPIRITUAL SEARCHING

Deprived of the luxury of continued schooling, Allen turned to the next best thing: books. He read voraciously in his spare hours, seeking solace and inspiration in the written word. The libraries and bookshops of Victorian Leicester became his true alma mater. Through the works of Shakespeare, the Bible, and the philosophers of East and West, he began to piece together his own vision of life's purpose. Emerson, Carlyle, Tolstoy, and Buddhist scriptures all left a mark on the young Allen's mind. He became convinced that the roots of happiness and suffering lay not in external events, but within the mind and heart.

The hard years in the offices and factories also fostered in Allen a deep empathy for the working class, a firsthand understanding of the grind of ordinary life, and a belief in the dignity of labor. He was no idle dreamer—his feet remained firmly planted on the ground, even as his thoughts reached for the heights. "Circumstances do not make the man," he would later write, "they reveal him." This maxim would become the quiet engine behind all his work.

MARRIAGE AND LITERARY BEGINNINGS

In 1895, at the age of 31, Allen married Lily Louisa Oram, a woman whose steadfastness and gentle encouragement would prove central to his later achievements. The couple moved first to South Wales and then to Ilfracombe, a seaside village in Devon that became the setting for Allen's most creative years. It was Lily who encouraged James not only to pursue his literary ambitions, but also to publish his now-famous meditations on thought and character.

Allen's first book, *From Poverty to Power* (1901), signaled his emergence as a serious thinker in the field of personal development. Drawing from his own experiences of hardship, the book offered readers a blend of practical wisdom and spiritual aspiration. Its modest success emboldened Allen to write more, and soon he was publishing a steady stream of essays, booklets, and meditations—all self-funded, distributed by post, and read by a growing, if still niche, audience.

AS A MAN THINKETH: THE BREAKTHROUGH

The publication of *As a Man Thinketh* in 1903 would change everything, though not immediately. According to family lore, Allen was dissatisfied with the manuscript, fearing it was too slight and simple. It was Lily who recognized the quiet power of the work and persuaded him to send it to press. The book, small enough to fit in a pocket, was priced affordably so that "thoughtful people" of all classes could read it.

What Allen may not have realized at first was that this brief treatise distilled, with rare clarity, the philosophy he had spent years living and pondering. Its central idea—that we become what we think—spoke directly to the era's hunger for both personal agency and spiritual meaning. Letters from readers soon began to arrive, thanking Allen for his insight and encouragement.

THE PHILOSOPHER OF ILFRACOMBE

For the rest of his life, Allen continued to write with remarkable discipline. He rose at dawn, spent his mornings in study and contemplation, and wrote in the afternoons. He maintained a simple routine, favoring walks along the Devon cliffs, tending to his garden, and engaging in quiet charity. He and Lily lived modestly, eschewing luxury for the contentment of a purposeful life. Friends and neighbors remembered Allen as gentle, unassuming, and deeply principled—a man who practiced the serenity and self-mastery he preached.

Between 1903 and his death in 1912, Allen published nearly twenty books and pamphlets, including *Above Life's Turmoil*, *Byways of Blessedness*, and *The Mastery of Destiny*. While none achieved the enduring popularity of *As a Man Thinketh*, each was marked by the same clarity, humility, and earnest desire to be of service.

LEGACY AND ENDURING INFLUENCE

James Allen died unexpectedly at the age of 47, having lived just long enough to see his words take root in the minds of a growing circle of admirers. He was buried in Ilfracombe, in the landscape that had become his spiritual home. In the years that followed, *As a Man Thinketh* would outgrow its modest origins, inspiring countless readers worldwide and helping to shape the burgeoning self-help movement of the twentieth century.

If Allen himself receded into quiet obscurity, his book did the opposite, quoted by leaders, coaches, and ordinary people striving for meaning in every corner of the globe. The power of his message—rooted in lived experience, hardship overcome, and the lifelong work of thought—remains undimmed by time.

James Allen's life, in the end, is his greatest testimony. He lived the truth he taught: that greatness is not the result of circumstance, but of the character shaped, day by day, in the crucible of one's own thoughts.

THIS RESTORED EDITION OF *As a Man Thinketh*
WAS COMPLETED IN JUNE 2025, COINCIDING WITH
NATIONAL ATTITUDE DAY (JUNE 5TH), A
CELEBRATION OF POSITIVITY AND
INTENTIONAL MINDSET.

THE TIMING IS FITTING FOR A WORK
THAT HIGHLIGHTS THE PROFOUND TRUTH:
THOUGHTS SHAPE CHARACTER AND DESTINY.